They lived like this in
ANCIENT CHINA

Author: MARIE NEURATH

Artist: JOHN ELLIS

of the Isotype Institute

FRANKLIN WATTS INC
575 Lexington Avenue, New York 22

© 1966 Isotype Institute Limited
Printed in Great Britain by Cox & Wyman Ltd

Library of Congress Catalog No. AC 67—10000

ANCIENT CHINA

At the time when the Romans believed that they ruled most of the world, another powerful empire existed. The Romans knew about a country from which they got the highly cherished material silk; for want of another name they called it 'the land of silk'. It was only generations later that more about this country, China, became known in the West.

China already had a longer history than Rome. There were books which told about many generations of rulers.

Since then, objects have been found buried in the ground near the Yellow River, where towns and temples once stood.

Some of these objects are more than 3,000 years old. Among them are bronze vessels which were used in ceremonies. Those with three legs are called tripods.

3

The ornament on the tripod on the previous page was often used as decoration in those early times. It is in the shape of a face.

You can see the two eyes with eyebrows above and the nose in the middle.

Another common shape looks like a snake or scorpion. It is a dragon, an imaginary animal.

Dragons were honoured as good spirits which brought rain.

Sometimes the mask looks like two dragons facing each other.

This curly pattern, found on
many surfaces, is known as
the cloud pattern.

Another, which covers whole
areas with spiral shapes, is
called the thunder pattern.

Early ornaments were believed to have power to influence the gods
and spirits. Like religious ceremonies, they pleased the spirits
which brought rain and good crops.

Sometimes human figures were used.

The Chinese learned bronze-making from other tribes, and they soon
became very accomplished. They also learned pottery from their
neighbours, and finally became the best potters of the world.

In very early times their pottery
was thick and hard with a shiny
glaze all over the painted surface.
Later, by using special materials
they invented porcelain, or real
'china'. It is delicate, thin and
can almost be seen through.
People all over the world learned
this art from China.

Pictures made in early
times show how the
people lived.
In this hunting scene
men are using spears.

In other pictures men are
shown with bows and arrows.
One is shooting water-fowl.
The water is full of fish.

Another has his arrow
attached to a string,
so that he can retrieve it.

This is a musical scene from a bronze vessel. A pole, supported by
two bird-like shapes, carries four bells and five sounding-stones
or gongs. The people, who beat them with hammers, are underneath.
The bells are probably made of bronze, and the gongs of jade, a
very hard and highly valued stone used for carved ornaments.

Other early pictures, painted on tiles, show farmers at work,
cutting, gathering and threshing the grain.

The people in the north grew millet and wheat, and in the warmer
wet south, rice was the main crop. The Chinese were the first people
to grow oranges, peaches, cane sugar and tea.

Horses were brought to China in early times. This horse-drawn chariot appears in one of the hunting scenes decorating an early bronze vessel.

Throughout the ages Chinese artists liked to draw horses. A later scene from a painted tile shows a chariot and horsemen side by side. The chariot wheels have many spokes.

In early warfare the nobles rode in chariots while the soldiers followed on foot. Later all the men were mounted on horseback, forming cavalry. Their enemies in the grassland to the north-west of China were also horsemen. The Chinese, looking for allies against these invaders, who were a great nuisance, discovered people in Central Asia who had better, stronger horses. They succeeded in getting these fine horses, and brought foreign grooms to take care of them.

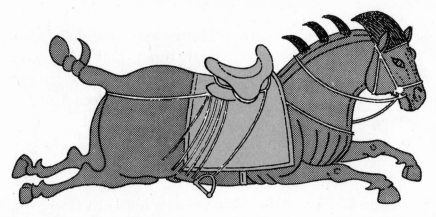

Some centuries later, this horse, wounded in war, was painted on the wall of a tomb. It shows a Chinese invention, the stirrup.

Another Chinese invention was the collar harness. This is much better than the harness the Romans used, as it does not press against the horse's throat and hamper its breathing.

The Chinese were also the first to use a wheelbarrow with one wheel, pushed by a man. Sometimes, by attaching a sail to it, they used the wind to help move the load.

China became united under emperors, who lived secluded in their splendid palaces. There were towns, too, but everything was built of wood and clay, and nothing has survived. Only a few pictures show what they were like. Here is part of a house with a straight roof, and a tower or gate at its side.

But we can still see one impressive work, the greatest building project that men ever conceived. The emperors made thousands of people labour for long years to build the Great Wall of China against

the mounted invaders. It is hundreds of miles long, made of earth faced with brick, and has castellations and watch-towers. It is still more or less intact after 2,000 years. The people hated this forced labour. Perhaps that is why they drew no pictures of the wall. The monumental gateway shown here is of the same period. Facing south, it carries the phoenix, a symbol of the sun and of good luck.

The Chinese did not rely only on fighting men and walls for protection. By prayer and ceremony the emperor asked the help of the sun and earth gods, and of his own ancestors. Magic and divining, with the help of this ancient sign, were also used.

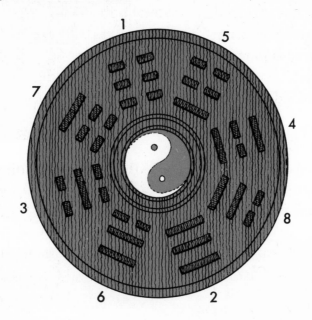

The eight symbols stand for 1 and 2 earth and heaven, 3 and 4 water and fire, 5 and 6 thunder and wind, 7 and 8 mountains and vapour. They are all different though composed out of only two signs:

▦ ▦ which stands for darkness, earth or female,
▬ which stands for brightness, heaven or male.
These are also called the Yin and the Yang.

The symbol in the centre stands for the interaction of the Yin and the Yang.

The Chinese tried to find out the gods' wishes through oracles.

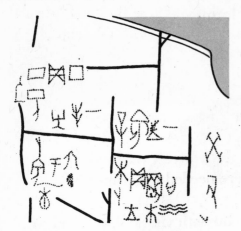

They wrote their questions on bones or tortoise shells. These were heated in a special way, so that cracks formed whose position among the words gave the answers. Often these were then also written on the shell. These writings are among the oldest that have been found in China.

A few written signs had already been made on bronze vessels:

When words were scratched on bone, the shape of the signs changed:

Later, the lines became more flowing when brushes and ink were used for writing:

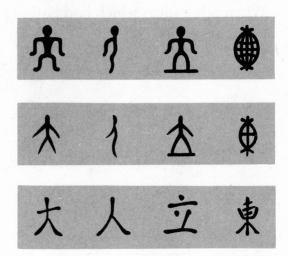

In each case the signs stand for 'great', 'man', 'to stand', and 'the east'. Written signs had the same meaning throughout China, though the spoken words for them differed according to the local language.

There are many more signs on the bone oracles than on bronze vessels. Here are some of them, with their later forms:

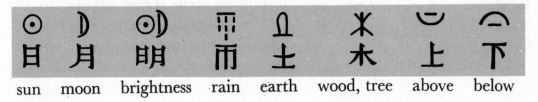

sun   moon   brightness   rain   earth   wood, tree   above   below

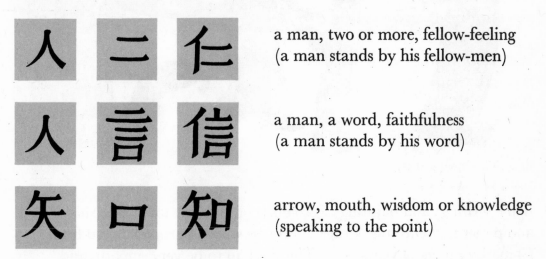

The sign for 'metal' combines the signs for roof and earth. It represents a mine, as mines were needed to get metals.

When other ideas which had nothing to do with visible things had to be expressed in books, new combinations were invented:

a man, two or more, fellow-feeling
(a man stands by his fellow-men)

a man, a word, faithfulness
(a man stands by his word)

arrow, mouth, wisdom or knowledge
(speaking to the point)

Knowledge and education were valued highly. In her greatest years China was ruled by scholars, and even lowly-born men could achieve high office if they passed the public examinations.

These scholars studied Chinese history, and early poetry written about the same time as the Psalms in the Bible. Kung Fu-tzu, or Confucius, the wise teacher, urged men to read the old poetry and learn from it how to lead a good life; he taught them to follow the old rules, respect their family, worship their ancestors and obey their rulers. His followers preserved the old books.

Some writings and paintings were done on the new materials, silk and paper made from silk rags, a process which Europe learned from China hundreds of years later. The silk had to be very smooth, and here we see how this was done. A piece of silk slung around two rods is being stretched by two women. Another smoothes the surface with a flat iron while a girl helps her to stretch the material crosswise.

Charcoal for the flat iron is kept glowing in a drum. A girl is keeping the fire going by moving a fan. Near her sits a woman with a piece of material on her knees, as though she is sewing. Silk had many uses, and she may be making a dress.

From early times, silk was also exported.

The silk trade was flourishing when the Chinese Empire spread its rule far to the south and the west. In addition to the Yellow River, China now included the land around the great Yangtse River and the West River farther south. Along the Yangtse River the farmers grew rice, tea and the mulberry tree on whose leaves the silkworms fed. The silk traders travelled west to the frontiers of the Chinese Empire. They sold their silk to traders of the neighbouring country who benefited greatly from their role as middlemen, so they took care that the Romans and Chinese never met.

Using ink on soft materials Chinese scribes and painters could not make any corrections. When they made a mistake they had to start all over again, so a sure hand was needed. They became masters of the delicate brushstroke, both in calligraphy (the art of writing) and in painting, for which they used very little colour.

These paintings depict the vast landscapes of the country. There were steep mountains in the west. Often bare, they had weathered to strange shapes.

Some of the rivers coming from the mountains sometimes crossed wide plains which they flooded. The Yellow River even changed its course. Huge dykes and canals were built to control the water.

Boats had many shapes and many uses, like transport and fishing. Some families lived on their barges. On fast moving streams the boats were steered through the rapids with great skill.

Where the ground was hard enough, roads could be built for carts, pulled by oxen or horses. Men and animals rested at this mountain inn and were fed. As you can see, camels were also used.

Bridges were built across the streams.

Made of stone or wood, they had many shapes.

This long wooden bridge across a wide river is used by men on foot
and others on horseback. A loaded ferry is being pulled across.
On softer ground, through streams and marshes, the most usual
transport was by water buffalo. Here the shepherd on the old
buffalo looks back to make sure that the young one is following.

The rice fields were
surrounded by dykes. After
ploughing, sowing and planting,
the fields were kept under
water. In the scene below
the harvest is being
gathered.

The cut plants are put
on wooden stands to dry.

Afterwards they are threshed
in the farmyard.

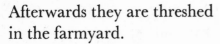

Some men are winnowing,
while others, using hammers
of wood or stone, pound
the grain in a mortar.
Four men push a long rod
to grind the rice between
the millstones.

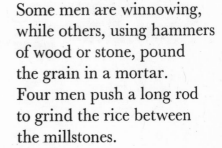

The drawings on these two pages are taken from a painting made
nearly a thousand years ago. Most of the drawings on the following
pages are from the same time.

A belt of wooden paddles
in a trough is used
to lift water from the
river to the fields.
It is turned by the
men's feet on the treads
of the rod.

The Chinese also knew how to make animals work for them. Here a
buffalo turns a wheel which works a similar water-lifting device.

The Chinese invented many machines but their paintings do not always
explain how they worked. Most painting was done from memory, and
technical details, in which a painter perhaps had little interest,
might be wrong or missing.

In this picture the artist showed how a horizontal water-wheel was used to open and close a leather bag like a concertina. The bag is a sort of bellows which forces air through a blast furnace in which iron is smelted.

There were no large factories. Small blast furnaces worked by a few men were scattered over the country near villages and towns. They provided material for the blacksmiths and ironmongers, wheelwrights and swordmakers.

Kinsmen lived together in fenced compounds, married sons with their
parents and grandparents. Each family had its own courtyard.
This is a scholars' compound near a river with its rice-field. A few
steps lead to the tiled house, raised on a platform under shady trees.
Here the scholar works in his quiet retreat. A boat is tied to the
river bank.

24

In later years the towns teemed with people. There were craftsmen, labourers and farmers. The rich traders and high officials kept great houses with many servants. Here is a street with the entrance and first courtyard of a fine house. In style it has the same wooden pillars as in early times, but the roof shows the curve characteristic of later buildings.

These buildings also show how the roof corners turned upwards. Their windows overlook the river, where dragon boats are taking part in a race. It is the Dragon Boat Festival, a time of merrymaking for everyone.

The Chinese had no regular rest days each week, but there were many popular festivals. The New Year was celebrated with fireworks and decorated lanterns.

This picture shows a public procession with music and dancers.

Jugglers show their skill, and athletes perform on top of a pole which is carried on a strong man's forehead. Even today Chinese acrobats show great skill in their dances and other performances.

A Chinese painter would sit in quiet contemplation of a scene, as this man does – so still that even the bird is not aware of his presence. Later, at home, he would re-create the scene from memory in his picture.

Other men also practised contemplation.
They were guided by the teaching of
great thinkers like Lao-tzu, whose
picture you see here. He is said to
have lived even earlier than Confucius.

While living by Confucian rules, men also followed Lao-tzu in
retiring for a time for quiet contemplation, so both teachings
could be followed side by side.

Buddhism, which came from India, also taught meditation, and belief in life after death. Building pagodas like this was one way of showing faith.

Holy men like this monk lived in monasteries. Their temples were filled with works of art. Scenes and statues carved in stone told the stories of their religion.

The teachings of Confucius and Lao-tzu were never carried to other countries. But Buddhism spread far. Missionaries explained Buddhism in words and pictures which they cut into wooden blocks, and printed.

These were the first prints made on paper anywhere. The Chinese also invented movable type, although it could not easily be used for their writing with its thousands of signs.

30

The Chinese invented gunpowder. They used it for fireworks which they enjoyed. They also invented the compass.

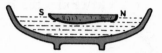

This magnetic fish floating in a dish of water pointed south. It was used to find out which way temples, tombs or thrones should face.

This sea-going sailing ship is called a 'junk' and has been used by the Chinese for hundreds of years.

They knew the constellations of stars. But in spite of their advanced knowledge they were not the first to sail around the earth.

Conquerors invaded their country at various times. Tartars conquered and ruled them, but soon adopted Chinese ways. The Mongols destroyed the northern lands, which never recovered. Yet even the Mongols learned to respect the Chinese culture, and did not destroy the south. The Yangtse River area then became the centre of Chinese life. From it a new dynasty arose which drove the Mongols out and led in a new, flourishing era.

China proper, which the Chinese themselves called 'the Middle Kingdom', still has the same ancient eighteen provinces which fall into three groups around its three great rivers, the Yellow River in the north, the Yangtse in the centre, and the West River in the south.

For centuries the many millions of Chinese people who live in these lands, speaking different languages, have been held together by a common writing, the same great traditions of art, and the wisdom of their learned men.